MW00905197

YOUNG WINNERS' GUIDE TO THE 'BIG BOOK'

JOHN ROSENGREN

CompCare Publishers

2415 Annapolis Lane
Minneapolis, Minnesota 55441

ISBN 0-89638-209-5

Cover design by Jeremy Gale
Interior design by Nancy MacLean

Inquiries, orders, and catalog requests should be addressed to
CompCare Publishers
2415 Annapolis Lane
Minneapolis, Minnesota 55441
Call toll free 800/328-3330
(Minnesota residents 612/559-4800)

 5 . 4 3   2   1
94 93 92 91 90

Author's Introduction

If necessity is the mother of invention, she is the matriarch of this guide to *Alcoholics Anonymous*, AA's Big Book, which is the cornerstone for Twelve Step Recovery Programs.

While working as a counselor in a treatment center for teenage drug abusers, I wanted the kids to read the Big Book for all its wisdom and inspiration. The problem? A lot of kids didn't want to read the Big Book. It was *too* big, they said. Too old-fashioned. There was too much in it about older people.

My challenge was to find a simple way to show young recovering people how the book's stories and suggestions related to their own lives. The answer was this workbook/guide.

Worksheets, which apply to the book's separate chapters and stories, connect old-timers' experiences to those of kids today. They show definitively how an alcoholic or other drug addict can be any age, sex, race, ethnic background, or religion. Chemical dependency is, as they say, an equal opportunity disease. When recovering kids were assigned short reading assignments—a chapter or story in the Big Book—along with the related worksheet, they did them. Even kids who said they didn't like to read started doing their assignments.

The worksheets turned out to be thought-provoking exercises for young people who weren't yet allowed to leave the unit to attend outside AA, who were working on their Steps, or who had questions about spirituality.

Sometimes these kids in treatment shared in group what they had learned by doing the worksheets. Sometimes we talked together individually.

Now the same worksheets, which proved to be so useful for young, recovering clients, have been compiled into this book, *Young Winners' Guide to the Big Book*.

But a teenager doesn't have to be in treatment to use this guide. He or she can be considering treatment, participating in aftercare, or recovering in AA or Narcotics Anonymous or another Twelve Step group. Nor does a person have to be a teenager to do them. This guide will work for anyone interested in getting to know the Big Book better. It can help anyone find and apply the "experience, strength, and hope" of AA's Program.

The exercises in this guide can be completed consecutively, or at random. A reader can choose to do just one, a few, or all of them.

The richness of recovery is there for anyone, of any age, in the Big Book.

John Rosengren

Editor's Preface

This companion guide to *Alcoholics Anonymous*, AA's Big Book, helps to bridge the two-generation gap between the 1930s, when the book was written, when alcoholics were mostly male and well past adolescence, and the present.

According to the National Clearinghouse for Alcohol and Drug Information, 10.3 percent of those now treated for alcoholism and other drug dependency are under the age of 18. Most of these are polydrug users; that is, they do not use only alcohol, although alcohol is the drug most often used.

Still, in spite of the relative youth of many of today's alcoholics/chemical dependents, and the complicating factor of today's other mind-altering drugs like cocaine (including crack), the wisdom of the Big Book holds. As it did in 1935 and has continued to do in ensuing years, the Big Book guides recovering people to examine their own alcohol and other drug use and learn the foundations of sobriety.

By allowing *Young Winners' Guide to the Big Book* to help them along the way, young people discover that AA's classic, written by people in their grandparents' generation, has something important to say to them today. When it comes to addiction and principles of recovery, there IS no generation gap!

As the Big Book concludes its text:

"May God bless you on the Road of Happy Destiny."

About the Big Book:

"It's like a big meeting all in one book. What's in the book applies to us fifty years later—that's really cool."
Jackie, nineteen, with one and a half years of sobriety

Chapter 1

'Bill's Story'

Read chapter 1 and answer the following questions:

1. *Complete this sentence*: "Liquor ceased to be a luxury; it became a _____."
(P. 5) What did this mean for Bill W.?

_____

_____

_____

_____

2. On page 8, Bill confesses: "Alcohol was my master." What, exactly, did he mean?

_____

_____

_____

_____

_____

3. Though once a successful businessman, Bill had many consequences from his drinking:

- arguments with friends about how much he drank (P. 3),
- blown job opportunities (P. 5),
- stealing money from his wife for alcohol (P. 6),
- hospitalization (P. 7),
- hangovers that left him feeling remorse, horror, and hopelessness (P. 6),
- and eventually feelings of loneliness and despair (P. 8).

What are some of the consequences you had from drinking and using?

1. _____

_____

2. _____

_____

3. _____

_____

4. _____

_____

5. _____

_____

4. Bill did not want the consequences to continue. He tried to quit on his own, but couldn't (Pp. 5-8). Have you ever tried to quit on your own?_____

How long was it before you started using again?

_____

5. Bill's friend told Bill that "God had done for him what he could not do for himself." (P. 11) What was that?_____

_____

6. What did Bill have to do to get what his friend had? (P. 12)

_____

_____

_____

_____

_____

_____

_____

_____

7. In the hospital, Bill said a prayer to God and did not take a drink again in his lifetime. (P. 13) *Match his actions in the left column with the corresponding steps of AA in the right column*:

A. "Humbly offered myself to God...to do with me as He would." "Placed myself unreservedly under his care and direction."

B. "Admitted...that of myself I was nothing; that without Him I was lost."

C. "Ruthlessly faced my sins."

D. "Became willing to have my new-found Friend take them [my sins] away."

E. Fully acquainted my schoolmate "with my problems and deficiencies."

F. "Made a list of people I had hurt...."

G. "I was to sit quietly when in doubt, asking only for direction and strength to meet my problems as He would have me."

1. "We admitted we were powerless over alcohol—that our lives had become unmanageable."

3. "Made a decision to turn our will and our lives over to the care of God *as we understood Him*."

4. "Made a searching and fearless moral inventory of ourselves."

5. "Admitted to God, to ourselves, and to another human being the exact nature of our wrongs."

6. "Were entirely ready to have God remove all these defects of character."

8. "Made a list of all persons we had harmed, and became willing to make amends to them all."

11. "Sought through prayer and meditation to improve our conscious contact with God, *as we understood Him*, praying only for knowledge of His will for us and the power to carry that out."

8. What were the essential requirements for Bill to have a way of living that answered all his problems? (Pp. 13-14)

1. _____

_____

2. _____

_____

3. _____

_____

4. _____

_____

9. *Fill in the blanks.* Through his work with other alcoholics, Bill said, "We commenced to make many fast _____ and a _____ has grown up among us of which it is a _____ thing to feel a part. The _____ of living we really have, even under pressure and difficulty." (P. 15)

Chapter 2

'There Is a Solution'

Read chapter 2 and answer the following questions:

1.   What is the "great news" this book carries to those who suffer from alcoholism? (P. 17)

_____

_____

2.   "With the alcoholic illness...there goes annihilation of all things worthwhile in life." What kinds of destruction does the book list? (P. 18)

   1. _____

   2. _____

   3. _____

What are some of the "worthwhile" things drinking/using destroyed in your life?

1. _____
   _____
2. _____
   _____
3. _____
   _____

3. "At some stage of his drinking career, he [the real alcoholic] begins to lose all control of his liquor consumption, once he starts to drink." What does the book say it means for the alcoholic to "lose all control"? How does losing control affect his behavior? (P. 21)

_____
_____
_____
_____
_____
_____
_____
_____
_____
_____

4. "Once [an alcoholic] takes any alcohol whatever into his or her system, something happens, both in the bodily and mental sense, which makes it virtually impossible to stop drinking." (P. 22) *List times when you drank or used other drugs more than you meant to drink or use*:

1. _____

_____

2. _____

_____

3. _____

_____

5. *Complete this sentence:* The main problem of the alcoholic centers in the _____, rather than in the _____. (P. 23)

6. "There is a solution." What is it? *Circle the answer from page 25.*
   A. Ignore all this and keep using.
   B. Accept spiritual help.
   C. Quit on your own.

7. *Complete the sentence:* "This [accepted spiritual help] we did because we _____ wanted to, and were _____." (P. 26)

8

8. "A new life has been given us or, if you prefer, 'a design for living' that really works." (P. 28) What would you like from a "new life"?

_____

_____

_____

_____

9. *Complete this sentence*: "He [God] has commenced to accomplish those things for us which _____

_____
(P. 25)

─────────

"Sobriety is a journey. The Big Book acts as a tour guide along that journey; the Steps show the way along the path."
Andrea, nineteen, with six months of sobriety

─────────

Chapter 3

'More about Alcoholism'

Read chapter 3 and answer the following questions:

1.   Page 31 describes some of the methods we tried to prove we could drink like others and didn't have a problem. What are some of the ways you tried to use "normally" to show you didn't have a problem?

   1. _____

      _____

   2. _____

      _____

   3. _____

      _____

   4. _____

      _____

   5. _____

2. *Complete this sentence*: "Commencing to drink after a period of sobriety, _____."
(P. 33)

3. "Once an alcoholic, always an alcoholic." (P. 33) What does this mean to you?_____

_____

_____

_____

4. "For those who are unable to drink moderately, the question is how to stop altogether." How does anyone stop drinking altogether? (P. 34)

_____

_____

_____

5. What was Jim's downfall? (Pp. 36-37) What would you have told him to stop him from making this mistake?

_____

_____

_____

6. How was your life like the jaywalker's? (Pp. 37-38)

_____

_____

_____

_____

_____

7. *Complete this sentence*: "The actual or potential alcoholic, with hardly an exception, _____

_____

_____." (P. 39)

8. Where must our defense not to drink come from? (P. 43)

_____

"The Big Book gave me some guidelines to progress. It gave me room to be myself. And it showed me the way to sobriety and serenity."

Ken, eighteen, with three years of sobriety

Chapter 4

'We Agnostics'

Read Chapter 4 and answer the following questions:

1. According to the Big Book, you know you are probably alcoholic if:

   1. _____

     _____

   2. _____

     _____

2. *Fill in the blank*: The Big Book calls alcoholism an illness which only a_____ will conquer. (P. 44)

3. *Complete these sentences*: "Much to our relief, we discovered_____
_____
_____."

"Our own conception, however inadequate, was

_____
_____."(P. 46)

How does this explain the phrase from Step
Eleven, "God as we understood Him"?

_____

_____

_____

_____

4. People are on their way as soon as they do what?
(P. 47) _____

_____

_____

5. What are the three spiritual handicaps the Big
Book lists? (P. 48)

    1. _____

    2. _____

    3. _____

What are some of the traits that have handicapped
you spiritually?

_____

_____

_____

_____

_____

_____

6. What is the one proposition that the men and women of AA have agreed upon? (P. 50)

_____

_____

_____

7. Since they came to believe in a Power greater than themselves and have done certain simple things, what have these men and women found? (P. 50)

_____

_____

_____

_____

_____

8. Pages 53-54 talk about some of the things we worshipped, believed in, or loved that were beyond reason or proof. *List several things you worshipped, believed in, or loved.*

1. _____

2. _____

3. _____

4. _____

   _____

   _____

   _____

9. *Complete this sentence*: "Deep down in every man, woman, and child is_____ _____." (P. 55) *List times when you have been aware of this fundamental idea of God.*

1. _____
   _____

2. _____
   _____

3. _____
   _____

10. *Complete this sentence*: According to the Big Book, God "has come to all who_____ _____." (P. 57)

When does God disclose Himself? (P. 57)_____
_____
_____

"I was having trouble with the idea of a Higher Power, so I read 'We Agnostics.' The chapter gave me something to work with—solid ground to start on. When I'm working one of the Steps, the Big Book explains the Step to me. Sometimes during the day I just open the book up and start reading. It doesn't matter where I open it, there's always something that jumps out for me to use."

Vivian, seventeen, with nine months of sobriety

Chapter 5

'How It Works' Part I

Read to the end of (a), (b), and (c) on page 60 and answer the following questions:

1. What keeps some people from recovering? (P. 58)

_____

_____

_____

2. Recovery is a manner of living that demands rigorous honesty. Is there an easier, softer way? (P. 58)

_____

_____

3. Some have tried to hold on to their old ideas. Did this work? _____ What did they have to do? (P. 58)

_____

_____

_____

4. What does the book mean when it says that alcohol is "cunning, baffling, powerful"? (Pp. 58-59)

_____

_____

_____

5. *Fill in the blanks*: "Half measures availed us _____. We stood at the turning point. We asked His protection and care with _____." (P. 59)

6. *Number the Steps.* (Pp. 59-60)

____ Admitted to God, to ourselves, and to another human being the exact nature of our wrongs.

____ Made a searching and fearless moral inventory of ourselves.

____ Having had a spiritual awakening as a result of these steps, we tried to carry this message to alcoholics, and to practice these principles in all our affairs.

____ We admitted we were powerless over alcohol—that our lives had become unmanageable.

____ Continued to take personal inventory and when we were wrong promptly admitted it.

____ Made a decision to turn our will and our lives over to the care of God as we understood Him.

____ Came to believe that a power greater than ourselves could restore us to sanity.

____ Made a list of all persons we had harmed, and became willing to make amends to them all.

____ Humbly asked Him to remove our shortcomings.

____ Were entirely ready to have God remove all these defects of character.

____ Made direct amends to such people wherever possible, except when to do so would injure them or others.

____ Sought through prayer and meditation to improve our conscious contact with God as we understood Him, praying only for knowledge of His will for us and the power to carry that out.

7. The Steps may seem a large order, but the Big Book says: "Do not be discouraged." What does it tell us to help us avoid discouragement? (P. 60)

_____

_____

_____

_____

8. *Fill in the blanks*: "We claim spiritual _____ rather than spiritual _____." (P. 60)

9. What are the three main ideas of this section? (P. 60)

1. _____

_____

2. _____

_____

3. _____

_____

'How It Works' Part II

Read from after the (a), (b), and (c) entries on page 60 to the last paragraph on page 63 and answer the following questions:

1. What is the first requirement of Step Three? (P. 60)

_____

_____

_____

2. "Most people try to live by self-propulsion. Each person is like an actor who wants to run the whole show. . . ." (P. 60) *List times you were like an actor trying to run the whole show.*

    1. _____

    _____

    2. _____

    _____

    3. _____

    _____

What happened?

_____

_____

_____

_____

_____

3. "Admitting he may be somewhat at fault, he is sure that other people are more to blame." (P. 61) *Give examples of times you blamed others:*

    1. _____

       _____

    2. _____

       _____

    3. _____

       _____

4. *Complete these sentences:* "So our troubles, we think, are basically _____
. . . Above everything, we alcoholics must be rid of _____. We must, or it _____ ." (P. 62)

5. "First of all, we had to quit playing God." (P. 62) Why? _____

6. What is the concept that was "the keystone of the new and triumphant arch through which we passed to freedom"? (P. 62)

_____

_____

_____

7. Page 63 offers an example of a prayer to say with the Third Step. *Write your own version of such a prayer, expressing your willingness to turn your will and life over to the care of God, as you understand God:*

_____

_____

_____

_____

_____

_____

_____

_____

_____

_____

_____

_____

*"The Big Book has always scared
me in a way. Maybe it's just too
real. Especially the part about
'self-will run riot'—that was me.
'We Agnostics' (Chapter Four of the
Big Book) helped me break out of
my shell and believe in a power
beyond myself. The book taught me
about being humble and that I can
learn from what other people have
to say. It's like a big meeting all in
one book. What's in the book
applies to us fifty years
later—that's really cool."*

Jackie, nineteen, one and a half years
sober

Chapter 5

'How It Works' Part III

Read from the last paragraph on page 63 to the last paragraph on page 68 and answer the following questions:

1. How must we take stock? (P. 64)

_____

2. What is the "number one" offender? (P. 64)

_____

3. What stems from resentment? (P. 64)

_____

4. *Complete this sentence:* "We have been not only mentally and physically sick, we have been_____

_____

_____." (P. 64)

5. *Following the example on page 66, list three people you resent, the cause, and how it affects you:*

I'm resentful at: The cause: Affects my:

1. _____   _____   _____

                    _____   _____

                    _____   _____

                    _____   _____

2. _____   _____   _____

                    _____   _____

                    _____   _____

                    _____   _____

3. _____   _____   _____

                    _____   _____

                    _____   _____

                    _____   _____

6. *Complete this sentence*: "It is plain that a life which includes deep resentment leads only to _____." (P. 66)

7. What does the Big Book suggest as a course to avoid resentment when offended? (Pp. 66-67)

_____

8. *Go back to the resentments you stated in No. 5 and show how you may have been at fault in each of the situations:*

1. _____
_____
_____

2. _____
_____
_____

3. _____
_____
_____

9. *Complete this sentence*: "We admitted our wrongs _____and were _____ to set these matters straight." (P. 67)

10. List three fears you have. (Pp. 67-68)

1. _____
_____

2. _____
_____

3. _____
_____

11. How does the Big Book suggest we begin to out-grow fear? (P. 68)

_____

_____

_____

_____

(We suggest you complete a more detailed Fourth Step. You may choose to use the guide on pages 78-80 of this workbook.)

Chapter 5

'How It Works' Part IV

Read from the last paragraph on page 68 to the end of the chapter and answer the following questions:

1. *Complete this sentence*: "We all have _____ problems. We'd hardly be human if we didn't." (P. 69)

2. *List times you were selfish, dishonest, or inconsiderate sexually.* (P. 69)

1. _____

_____

2. _____

_____

3. _____

_____

Whom have you hurt? _____

_____

_____

How have you unjustifiably aroused jealousy, suspicion, or bitterness? _____

_____

_____

_____

What could you have done instead? _____

_____

_____

_____

3. What is the test for each relationship? (P. 69)

_____

4. Whom do we ask to help us mold a sane and sound ideal of sex? (P. 69)_____

5. *Complete this sentence*: "We remembered always that our sex powers were _____ and therefore _____, neither to be used lightly or selfishly nor to be despised and loathed." (P. 69)

6. *Choose the correct answer to complete this sentence from page 69*: "Whatever our ideal turns out to be. . ."
    1. _____ we must be willing to grow toward it.
    2. _____ we must not tell anyone about it.
    3. _____ it is sure to be illegal.

7. Who is the final judge of our sex situation? (Pp.69-70)_____

8. *Complete this sentence*: "If we are not sorry, and our [sexual] conduct continues to harm others, we are _____ ." (P. 70)

9. Sum up what this section says about sex. (P. 70)

_____

_____

_____

_____

_____

_____

_____

_____

Chapter 6

'Into Action'

Read chapter 6 and answer the following questions:

1. What is the best reason for discussing ourselves with another person—that is, doing a Fifth Step? (P. 72)

_____

_____

2. *Complete this sentence*: "More than most people, the alcoholic _____." (P. 73)

Give examples of how you have led a double life:

1. _____
   _____
   _____

2. _____
   _____
   _____

3. _____
   _____
   _____

3. What must we do if we expect to live long or happily in this world? (Pp. 73-74)_____
_____
_____

4. *Complete this sentence*: Through the careful completion of the Steps, "We are building an arch through which we shall _____
_____." (P. 75)

5. The following is known as the Seventh Step Prayer. *Fill in the blanks.* "My Creator, I am now_____
that you should have all of me,_____.
I pray that you now _____
which stands in the way of _____
_____
Grant me _____ as I go out
from here, to do_____. Amen." (P. 76)

6. *Complete this sentence*: "Remember it was agreed at the beginning _____ _____." (P. 76)

7. Reminding ourselves that we have decided to go to any length to find a spiritual experience, what do we ask for? (P. 79)_____

_____

8. What do we ask our Creator each morning in meditation to show us? (P. 83)

_____

_____

9. What's the meaning of the statement: "The spiritual life is not a theory"? (P. 83)

_____

_____

10. On the bottom on page 83 and the top of page 84, the Big Book makes several promises of good things that will happen to us if we are painstaking in our spiritual housecleaning. *Pick out three that you would like to happen for yourself*:

    1. _____

    _____

    2. _____

    _____

    3. _____

    _____

11. With the Tenth Step, we need to continue to watch especially for certain defects. What are they? (P. 84)

_____

12. Our daily reprieve (relief) from alcoholism or chemical dependency is contingent (depends) on what? (P. 85)

_____

_____

13. When we retire at night, after making our review of the day, what do we do? (P. 86)

_____

_____

14. Before we begin our day, what do we ask God for? (P. 86)

_____

_____

_____

Chapter 7

'Working with Others'

Read chapter 7 and answer the following questions:

1. When talking with someone thinking of quitting, what would you say were the struggles that made you want to stop using? (P. 92)

_____

_____

_____

_____

_____

2. What does the Big Book mean by the "mental twist" that leads to drinking? (P. 92)

_____

_____

_____

3. What is the main thing needed by an alcoholic wanting to recover? (P. 93)

_____

_____

_____

_____

4. On page 94, it says "The more hopeless he [or she—the person you are trying to help] feels, the better."

Why is this? _____

_____

When did you feel hopeless? _____

_____

_____

_____

_____

5. *Complete this sentence*: "We have no monopoly on God; we merely _____

_____." (P. 95)

What does it mean not to have a monopoly on God?_____

_____

_____

_____

6. What is the foundation stone of recovery? (P. 97)

_____

7. *Complete this sentence*: "We simply do not stop drinking so long as we _____

_____

_____." (P. 98)

8. What is the only condition of getting well? _____
_____ (P. 98)

9. *Complete this sentence*: "When we look back, we realize that _____

_____

_____

_____

_____." (P. 100)

10. In regard to "slippery places" (as they are called in the little book, *A Day at a Time*), what does the Big Book tell us to be sure of before going to such places?

_____

_____

_____

_____

What would "slippery places" be for you?

_____

_____

_____

You can choose to "go or stay away." If you choose to go there, what would you need to do?

_____

_____

_____

_____

"For me, the Big Book's a guide to life. When I'm having a problem, I can pretty much find a solution to it in the book. I usually read it for some good serenity, to relax and be at peace with myself."

Sam, fifteen, six months sober

Chapter 8

'To Wives'

Read chapter 8 and answer the following questions:
(Note: Although what is said in this chapter is addressed to wives, it applies to families as well—parents, brothers, sisters, grandparents, and other important people who are close to us.)

1. *Complete this sentence*: "With few exceptions, our book thus far has spoken of men. But what we have said applies quite as much _____."
(P. 104)

2. *Complete this sentence*: Speaking for families, the Big Book says, "Had we fully understood the nature of the alcoholic illness,_____" (P. 107)

How does you help you understand some of your family members' actions?_____

_____

_____

_____

_____

_____

_____

3. *Complete this sentence*: "When drinking, they were
_____." (P. 107)
Some call this the Dr. Jekyll and Mr. Hyde effect, the
way our personality changes when drunk or high.
How were you a stranger to your family when using?

_____

_____

_____

4. Pages 108-110 describe four categories or stages
of drinking. Which one most closely describes your
use? *Explain how your use fit the symptoms described
in that category.*_____

_____

_____

_____

_____

_____

5. There were some alcoholics who seemed quite
hopeless. Everybody had given up on them. Yet, they
had what kind of recoveries? _____
(P. 113)

6. *Fill in the blank*: "Now we try to put spiritual
principles to work in _____
department of our lives." (P. 116)

7. What is the rule of families in recovery? (P. 118)

_____

8. *Fill in the blanks*: "You . . . ought to think of what
you can _____ life instead of how
much you can _____." (P. 120)

9. What does the Big Book say an alcoholic must do after a relapse in order to survive? (P. 120)_____

_____

10. In summary, what does this chapter suggest as a plan for families to live together in recovery?_____

_____

_____

_____

_____

Chapter 9

'The Family Afterward'

Read chapter 9 and answer the following questions:

1. What common ground should the family meet on? (P. 122)

_____

2. How do we learn from our experience and grow? (P. 124)

_____

_____

_____

_____

3. *Complete this sentence*: "As each member of a resentful family _____
_____
_____,

he lays a basis for helpful discussion." (P. 127)

What were some of your shortcomings with your family?

    1. _____

       _____

    2. _____

       _____

    3. _____

       _____

4. What will become the guiding principle in the family? (P. 128)_____

5. *Complete this sentence*: "We have found nothing incompatible between a _____
_____and a life
of _____." (P. 130)

6. *Fill in the blank*: "Each individual should consult his own _____." (P. 132) About what?_____
_____

7. What is the one thing we absolutely insist on? (P. 132)

_____

8. *Circle the correct answer to complete this sentence from page 132*: "Cheerfulness and laughter make for . . . ."

    1. idleness

    2. merriment

    3. usefulness

9. *Complete this sentence*: "We are sure God wants us to be _____." (P. 133)

10. What is a most powerful health restorative? (P. 133)

_____

11. What three mottoes are suggested for the family? (P.135)_____

_____

Chapter 10

'To Employers'

Read chapter 10 and answer the following questions:

1. The chapter begins with the stories of three suicides. (Pp. 136-137) The despair of alcoholism makes some want to kill themselves. Have you ever felt this kind of despair? How were these times related to your use?

_____

_____

_____

_____

2. Page 139 describes the alcoholic as brilliant, fast-thinking, imaginative, likeable, and hard-working when sober. What traits do you like about yourself when sober?

    1. _____

    2. _____

    3. _____

    4. _____

    5. _____

3. While drunk, the alcoholic often gets into scrapes that repulse him afterward. (P. 141) What kind of scrapes have you gotten into while drunk or high that you later wished hadn't happened?

1. _____

_____

2. _____

_____

3. _____

_____

4. *Complete this sentence*: "To get over drinking will require_____ _____."(P.143)

What does this mean?_____ _____ _____ _____

5. What are the greatest enemies of us alcoholics? (P. 145)_____ _____

6. In addition to work, what does one need to maintain one's sobriety? (P. 146)_____

7. *Complete this sentence*: "For he knows_____ _____ if he would live at all." (P. 146)

8. How is it that the two recovering alcoholic employees are able to produce as much as five normal salesmen? (Pp. 149-150)_____

_____

_____

_____

_____

Chapter 11

'A Vision for You'

Read chapter 11 and answer the following questions:

1. "There was always one more attempt [to control drinking and enjoy life as we did]—and one more failure." (P. 151) *Give examples of some things that you enjoyed about using when you first started, but that you lost in the later stages of your use.*

    1. _____
    _____

    2. _____
    _____

    3. _____
    _____

2. What is the substitute for alcohol and drugs? (P. 152)

_____

3. "There [in AA] you will find release from care, boredom and worry." (P. 152) This is one of the promises fulfilled for others in the fellowship. There are eight more on pages 152-153. *List them.*

1. _____

2. _____

3. _____

4. _____

5. _____

6. _____

7. _____

8. _____

4. *Complete this sentence*: "Since these things have happened among us,_____

_____." (P. 153)

5. What is "the old, insidious insanity"? Why? (P. 154)

_____

_____

6. "I've prayed to God on hangover mornings and sworn that I'd never touch another drop but by nine o'clock I'd be boiled as an owl." (P. 158) *Give examples of times you swore off using and soon after were drunk or high.*

    1. _____

       _____

    2. _____

       _____

    3. _____

       _____

7. Many have stepped over the threshold of home after the hospitalization into—what? (P. 160)
_____

8. What is it about AA that so many find irresistible? (P. 160)_____
_____
_____
_____
_____

9. In 1985, there were how many AA groups? _____

In how many countries?_____

With how many members? (P. 162)_____

10. Complete this sentence: "Abandon yourself _____

_____

_____

_____

_____." (P. 164)

'Doctor Bob's Nightmare'

Read the story and answer the following questions:

1. *Complete this sentence:* "My whole life seemed to be centered around _____ without regard for _____

_____

_____." (P. 172) What did your life center around? *Give examples:*_____

_____

_____

_____

_____

2. Dr. Bob's father tried several times to help him, but "this had little effect however for I kept on drinking ..." (P. 174) Who tried to help you quit?

_____

_____

_____

_____

3. Complete this sentence: "I drank with moderation at first, but it took me only a relatively short time to _____."
(P. 175) When have you tried to control your drinking and/or use?

    1. _____

    2. _____

    3. _____

4. Dr. Bob hid his supply of alcohol in the coal bin, the clothes chute, over door jambs, over beams in the cellar, in cracks in the cellar tile, in old trunks and chests, in the old can container, and in the ash container. Where did you hide your supply of alcohol or drugs?_____

_____

5. "I used to promise my wife, my friends, and my children that I would drink no more—promises which seldom kept me sober even through the day, though I was very sincere when I made them." (P. 177) Did you ever promise anyone, including yourself, that you would quit? _____ When?_____ What happened?_____

_____

6. What is the "beer experiment"? (Pp. 177-178)_____

_____

_____

7. The man who helped change Dr. Bob's life had experienced many years of frightful drinking, but had been cured by what? (P. 180)_____

_____

8. What was it about this man that made him different from others? (P. 180) _____

_____

_____

_____

9. Dr. Bob writes that for the first two and a half years of his sobriety he still craved a drink. But he didn't take one. (P. 181) What does this tell you? _____

_____

10. *Complete this sentence*: "It [the AA program] never fails, if _____

_____

_____

_____." (P. 181)

'He Had to Be Shown'

Read the story and answer the following questions:

1. The author's first drink, a martini, was repulsive to him. But he drank nine in half an hour. (P. 195) Why did he do this? Did you ever drink or use like this? When?_____

_____

_____

2. "All of a sudden I found myself guzzling." (P. 195) Why guzzle? When have you found yourself guzzling?

_____

_____

_____

3. "I early discovered that if I drank anything, I was not accountable for what happened." (P. 196) What does this mean?_____

_____

_____

4. "About that period, too, came increasing procrastination and the avoidance of responsibilities." (P. 197) List times you procrastinated (put things off) or avoided responsibility.

1. _____

2. _____

3. _____

5. Why did the author come to believe he was insane? (P. 199)_____

_____

6. *Complete this sentence:* "My big job was _____

_____

_____ ." (P. 199) Whom did you try to hide your crazy behavior from? _____

_____

_____

7. How come he hadn't been drunk for six months? (P. 200)

_____

_____

8. The author thought: "I could take one drink and get right back on the wagon." (P. 202) Was he right? What happened?_____

_____

_____

9. What did Dr. Bob tell the author when asked if he was going to want another drink? (Pp. 206-207)_____

_____

_____

10.   Complete this sentence: "The very simple program they advised me to follow was _____

_____

_____

_____

_____

_____." (Pp. 208-209)

'Women Suffer Too'

Read the story and answer the following questions:

1. When her friend suggested the author was drinking too much, what happened? (P. 226) Did you ever drop friends who did not approve of your drinking or use?

_____

_____

_____

2. After a while, drinking no longer gave her pleasure, it merely dulled the pain. (P. 226) How had you lost some of the pleasure of using?_____

_____

_____

_____

3. What caused the author to become a disillusioned cynic? (P. 226)_____

_____

4. How was alcohol a prop for her? (Pp. 226-227)____
_____
_____
_____

5. What was the revelation this woman found in reading the Big Book? (P. 227)_____

_____

6. Then she hit a snag. What was it? (P. 227)_____

_____

7. *Complete this sentence*: She overcame the snag when she realized "this wasn't 'religion'—this was _____!" (P. 228)

8. Salvation also means "to come home." How did the author find her salvation in AA? (P. 228)_____

_____
_____
_____

9. When and how did the feeling of impending disaster that had haunted this woman for years begin to dissolve? (P. 229)_____

_____
_____

They Stopped in Time

'Too Young'

Read the story and answer the following questions:

1.   This man thought "If I could lay off it (alcohol), that meant I didn't have to worry about a drinking problem." (P. 317) Was he right?_____

2.   The author quit school, then quit caring about his jobs in the army, but he didn't quit drinking. (Pp. 317-318) What did you quit before you quit using?

    1. _____

    2. _____

    3. _____

3.   "Everyone was against me—I'd show them I didn't need them." (P. 318) When have you felt like this?

_____

_____

_____

4.   Why did he think he couldn't be an alcoholic? (P. 319)

_____

5. He found out what all the people at the AA meeting wanted. (P. 320) What was it?_____

_____

6. When did AA give him a new life? (P. 320)_____

_____

_____

_____

They Stopped in Time

'Fear of Fear'

Read the story and answer the following questions:

1. What happened to this woman every time she drank? (P. 322)_____

2. Why didn't she drink in the morning? (P. 323)_____
_____

How did you try to avoid becoming an alcoholic or addict?_____
_____

3. Though the author did not lose many of the things other alcoholics lose, she lost something very important. What did she lose? (P. 323)_____
_____
_____

4. She felt a fear coming into her life. How did this fear affect her? (Pp. 323-324) _____
_____
_____

5. Sometimes drunk and sick, she would say the alcoholic's prayer: "Dear God, get me out of this one and I'll never do it again." (P. 324) When have you said this prayer, bargained with God to get you out of trouble?

1. _____

2. _____

3. _____

6. How has the author's relationship with her husband changed since she joined AA? (P. 325)_____

_____

_____

7. Why can't she afford resentments against anyone? (P. 325)_____

_____

8. What is this woman grateful for? (P. 326)_____

_____

_____

They Stopped in Time

'A Teenager's Decision'

Read the story and answer the following questions:

1. How did this girl drink? (P. 353)_____
_____

2. Why did alcohol seem to be the answer to all her problems? (P. 353)_____
_____

3. Was alcohol the answer to her problems? What problems did alcohol cause? (Pp. 353-355)
_____
_____
_____
_____

4. Once she started to hate herself, how did her drinking become a no-win cycle? (P. 354)
_____
_____
_____

5. What did the author know that made her call AA? (P. 355)_____

_____

6. What does she say is the only real freedom? What was the truth that set her free? (P. 355)_____

_____

7. Who is the only one who can take away her sobriety? How? (P. 355)_____

_____

They Lost Nearly All

'A Five-Time Loser Wins'

Read the story and answer the following questions:

1. *Complete this sentence:* "Intake of alcohol changes
_____." (P. 458) How did using
change your personality?_____
_____
_____

2. *Complete this sentence:* "With the first drink_____
_____
_____
_____." (Pp. 458-9)

3. How were we able to change our personality and
have a spiritual awakening? (P. 459)_____
_____

4. *Complete this sentence:* "All Twelve Steps of AA are
designed to _____ (deflate the old ego) and
_____." (P. 459)

5. *Complete this sentence:* " 'If you are an alcoholic and if you continue to drink, the end is death or insanity.' They hadn't mentioned _____
_____." (P. 461)

6. What did he do that allowed him to accept his plight? (P. 461) _____

7. "Being dry is not being sober." (P. 462) What does this mean? _____
_____
_____

8. To what does this man owe everything? (P. 463)
_____

9. *Complete this sentence:* "Guess I'll never be a saint, but whatever I am, _____
_____." (P. 463)

They Lost Nearly All

'Freedom from Bondage'

Read the story and complete the following questions:

1. *Complete this sentence:* "AA has taught me that through this simple program _____

_____

_____

_____

_____." (P. 544)

2. This woman got married twice in an attempt to change her surroundings and her life, but she still felt restlessness, anxiety, fear, and insecurity. (Pp. 545-546) Why is this? What did she need to change?

_____

_____

_____

3. *Complete this sentence:* "My basic problem was _____ ." (P. 546)

4. *Complete this sentence:* "In alcohol I found
_____ courage." (P. 547) How was this
courage false?

_____

_____

5. "With liquor I could always retire to my little
private world where nobody could get to me to hurt
me." (P. 547) How did you use alcohol and drugs to
avoid being hurt by others?_____

_____

_____

6. "Reality has two sides." What are they? The
_____ side and the _____ side (P. 550)

7. What does HOW stand for? (P. 550)
   H is for_____.
   O is for _____.
   W is for _____.

8. "These (honesty, openness, willingness) our Book
calls the essentials of recovery." *Complete this sentence:* "The application of these principles in our daily
lives will _____." (P. 550)

9. How did she know her life was unmanageable?
(P. 550)

_____

_____

10. Page 552 offers a suggestion for freedom from the bondage of resentment. *List three people you resent and can pray for:*

1. _____
2. _____
3. _____

11. Complete this sentence: "The only real freedom a human being can ever know is _____ _____." (P. 553)

'AA Taught Him to Handle Sobriety'

Read the story and answer the following questions:

1. *Complete this sentence:* "It's no great trick to stop drinking; the trick is _____." (P. 554)

2. By twenty-nine, the author was having trouble coping with life because of his drinking. What did he do to try to change things? (Pp. 555-556)

    1. _____

    2. _____

    3. _____

    4. _____

    5. _____

What are some of the things you tried—short of sobriety—to stop the problems you were having with your use?

1. _____

2. _____

3. _____

4. _____

5. _____

3. What grew with every drink he took? (P. 556)_____
_____

What are some of the lies you've told yourself?
_____
_____
_____
_____

4. When did he take refuge and comfort in alcohol? (P.556)_____

When did you take refuge and comfort in alcohol and other drugs? _____
_____
_____
_____
_____

5. Why was the author suffering such inner pain? (P. 557)_____
_____

6. Despite severe consequences (a damaged liver, cirrhosis, daily vomiting, blackouts, hemorrhages, near-death crises), this man kept drinking. (Pp. 557-558) Did you have some consequences that may have made others quit, but not you? What were they?

    1. _____

    2. _____

    3. _____

    4. _____

    5. _____

7. How do we learn to cope with the problems that we looked to booze or drugs to solve? (P. 560)

_____

_____

8. How do we cast off the burdens of the past and the anxieties of the future? (P. 560)_____

_____

9. *Fill in the blanks:* "We reject _____ and accept _____." (P. 560)

10. "AA does not teach us how to handle our drinking, it teaches us to handle sobriety." (P. 554) How did AA teach this man to handle his sobriety? (P. 559)

_____

_____

_____

"I've read all the stories. They've given me a view of the consequences adults faced and helped me realize the consequences I would face if I had stayed on the same path. The book proved to me that alcoholism is truly a disease and helped me believe that. Just the fact that there is a Big Book makes me feel I'm not alone—there are millions of copies out there."

Barry, seventeen, with nearly two years of sobriety

Fourth Step Guide

Following the instructions and example in pages 64-68 of the Big Book, complete this inventory:

I'm resentful at: _____

    Cause: _____

    Affects my: _____

    How I retaliated:_____

    _____

    _____

I'm resentful at: _____

    Cause: _____

    Affects my: _____

    How I retaliated:_____

    _____

    _____

I'm resentful at: _____

    Cause: _____

    Affects my: _____

    How I retaliated:_____

    _____

    _____

I'm resentful at: _____

    Cause: _____

    Affects my: _____

    How I retaliated:_____

    _____

    _____

I'm resentful at: _____

    Cause: _____

    Affects my: _____

    How I retaliated:_____

    _____

    _____

I'm resentful at: _____

    Cause: _____

    Affects my: _____

    How I retaliated:_____

    _____

    _____

I'm resentful at: _____
    Cause: _____
    Affects my: _____
    How I retaliated:_____
    _____
    _____

I'm resentful at: _____
    Cause: _____
    Affects my: _____
    How I retaliated:_____
    _____
    _____

I'm resentful at: _____
    Cause: _____
    Affects my: _____
    How I retaliated:_____
    _____
    _____

I'm resentful at: _____
    Cause: _____
    Affects my: _____
    How I retaliated:_____
    _____
    _____

Add extra pages of your own, if you need them.

Appendix 2

'Spiritual Experience'

Read the appendix and answer the following questions:

1. *Complete this sentence:* "The terms 'spiritual experience' and 'spiritual awakening' are used many times in this book, which shows ... that the personality change sufficient to bring about recovery from alcoholism has_____

_____

_____

_____." (P. 569)

2. What conclusion is erroneous? (P. 569)_____

_____

_____

3. *Complete this sentence:* "Most of our experiences are what the psychologist William James calls _____

_____." (P. 569)

4. *Complete this sentence:* "With few exceptions our members find that they have tapped _____

_____

_____

_____." (P. 570)

5. What do most of us think is the essence of spiritual experience? (P. 570)_____

_____

6. *Complete this sentence:* "Most emphatically we wish to say that any alcoholic capable of honestly facing his problems in the light of our experience can recover, provided _____

_____

_____ ." (P. 570)

7. What are the essentials of recovery? (P. 570)

_____

8. Herbert Spencer says "contempt prior to investigation" is "a bar against all information," "proof against all arguments," and keeps someone in everlasting ignorance. (P. 570) What does this mean?_____

_____

_____

_____

_____

_____

ANSWERS

CHAPTER 1 "Bill's Story"

1. necessity/he needed to drink to get through the day

2. it had overwhelmed him to the point of loneliness and despair

3. *personal*

4. *personal*

5. raised him to a level of life better than the best he'd ever known

6. be willing to believe in a power greater than himself; nothing more was required of him to make his beginning

7. A-3; B-1; C-4; D-6; E-5; F-8; G-11

8. belief in God/willingness/honesty/humility

9. friends/fellowship/wonderful/joy

CHAPTER 2 "There Is a Solution"

1. that we have discovered a common solution

2. it engulfs all whose lives touch the sufferer's/it brings misunderstanding, fierce resentment, financial insecurity, disgusted friends and employers/it warps lives of blameless children, sad wives and parents/*personal*

3. he can't control how he drinks; he does absurd, incredible, tragic things while drinking

4. *personal*

5. mind/body

6. accept spiritual help

7. honestly/willing to make the effort

8. *personal*

9. we could never do by ourselves

CHAPTER 3 "More about Alcoholism"

1. *personal*

2. we are in a short time as bad as ever

3. *personal*

4. on a spiritual basis

5. he thought just one drink on a full stomach wouldn't hurt/don't take the first drink

6. *personal*

7. will be absolutely unable to stop drinking on the basis of self-knowledge

8. a Higher Power

CHAPTER 4 "We Agnostics"

1. when you honestly want to, you find you cannot quit entirely/when drinking, you

have little control over the amount you take/

2. spiritual experience

3. "...we did not need to consider another's conception of God."/"...sufficient to make the approach and to effect a contact with Him."/God is not someone else's conception, but our own

4. "As soon as a man can say that he does believe, or is willing to believe, we emphatically assure him that he is on his way."

5. obstinacy, sensitiveness, unreasoning prejudice/*personal*

6. every one of them has gained access to, and believe in, a Power greater than himself

7. they found that a new power, peace, happiness and sense of direction flowed into them

8. *personal*

9. the fundamental idea of God/*personal*

10. "...all who have honestly sought Him."/when we drew near to Him

CHAPTER 5 "How It Works" PART 1

1. they cannot or will not completely give themselves to this simple program, usually men and women who are constitutionally incapable of being

honest with themselves

2. no

3. no/let go absolutely (of their old ideas)

4. we can't fight it alone

5. nothing/complete abandon

6. 5, 4, 12, 1, 10, 3, 2, 8, 7, 6, 9, 11

7. no one has been able to do it perfectly; we are not saints

8. progress/perfection

9. that we were alcoholic and could not manage our own lives/that probably no human power could have relieved our alcoholism/that God could and would if He were sought

CHAPTER 5 "How It Works" PART II

1. that we be convinced that any life run on self-will can hardly be a success

2. *personal*

3. *personal*

4. of our own making/this selfishness/kills us

5. it didn't work

6. God is the principal; we are His agents

7. *personal*

CHAPTER 5 "How It Works" PART III

1. honestly

2. resentment

3. all forms of spiritual disease

4. spiritually sick

5. *personal*

6. futility and unhappiness

7. to realize that the people who wronged us were perhaps spiritually sick and to ask God to help us show them tolerance, pity, and patience

8. *personal*

9. honestly/willing

10. *personal*

11. we ask God to remove our fear and direct our attention to what He would have us be

CHAPTER 5 "How It Works" PART IV

1. sex

2. *personal*

3. was it selfish or not?

4. God

5. God-given/good

6. 1. (we must be willing to grow toward it)

7. God

8. quite sure to drink

9. "We earnestly pray for the right ideal, for guidance in each questionable situation, for sanity, and for the strength to do the right thing."

CHAPTER 6 "Into Action"

1. if we skip this vital step, we may not overcome drinking

2. leads a double life/*personal*

3. we must be entirely honest

4. walk a free man

5. willing/good and bad/remove from me every single defect of character/my usefulness to you and my fellows/strength/your bidding

6. we would go to any lengths for victory over alcohol

7. that we be given strength and direction to do the right thing, no matter what the personal consequences may be

8. patience, tolerance, kindliness, and love

9. we have to live it

10. any three of the promises (Pp. 83-84)

11. selfishness, dishonesty, resentment, and fear

12. the maintenance of our spiritual condition

13. ask God's forgiveness and inquire what corrective measures should be taken

14. to direct our thinking, especially that it be divorced from self-pity, dishonest or self-seeking motives

CHAPTER 7 "Working with Others"

1. *personal*

2. the way the alcoholic mind can overcome our best intentions

3. the main thing is that he be willing to believe in a Power

greater than himself and that he live by spiritual principles

4. He will be more likely to follow your suggestions/*personal*

5. have an approach that worked with us/*personal*

6. helping others

7. place dependence upon other people ahead of dependence on God

8. that one trust in God and clean house

9. the things which came to us when we put ourselves in God's hands were better than anything we could have planned

10. be sure you are on solid ground before you start and that your motive is thoroughly good/*personal*

CHAPTER 8 "To Wives"

1. to women

2. we might have behaved differently/*personal*

3. strangers/*personal*

4 *personal*

5. spectacular and powerful

6. every

7. Live and Let Live.

8. put into/take out

9. redouble his spiritual activities

10. that each member work a spiritual program

CHAPTER 9 "The Family Afterward"

1. tolerance, understanding, and love

2. we grow by our willingness to face and rectify errors and convert them into assets

3. begins to see his shortcomings and admits them to others/*personal*

4. giving, rather than getting

5. powerful spiritual experience/sane and happy usefulness

6. conscience/religion

7. enjoying life

8. 3. (usefulness)

9. happy, joyous, and free

10. a spiritual mode of living

11. First Things First; Live and Let Live; Easy Does It

CHAPTER 10 "To Employers"

1. *personal*

2. *personal*

3. *personal*

4. a transformation of thought and attitude/we all had to place recovery above everything

5. resentment, jealousy, envy, frustration, fear

6. play

7. he must be honest

8. they have a new attitude, and they have been saved

from a living death

CHAPTER 11 "A Vision for You"

1. personal

2. fellowship in AA

3. your imagination will be fired/life will mean something at last/the most satisfactory years of your existence lie ahead/you are going to meet these new friends in your own community/among them you will make lifelong friends/you will be bound to them with new and wonderful ties/you will know what it means to give of yourself/you will learn the full meaning of "Love thy neighbor as thyself"

4. they can happen with you

5. that first drink/because it leads to another, and another, and another drunk

6. *personal*

7. freedom

8. the very practical approach to his problems, the absence of intolerance of any kind, the informality, the genuine democracy, the uncanny understanding

9. about 58,500 groups/in 114 countries/over 1,000,000 members

10. to God as you understand God

PIONEERS OF AA "Dr. Bob's Nightmare"

1. doing what I wanted to do/the rights, wishes, or privileges of anyone else/*personal*

2. *personal*

3. drift back into the old habits which had wound up so disastrously before/*personal*

4. *personal*

5. *personal*

6. drinking only beer in an effort to stop one's own problems with alcohol

7. the spiritual approach

8. he was the first person I'd talked with who knew about alcoholism from experience

9. he talked Dr. Bob's language

10. you go about it with half the zeal you have been in the habit of showing when you were getting another drink

PIONEERS OF AA "He Had to Be Shown"

1. because getting drunk was more important than taste/*personal*

2. *personal*

3. He lost control of his behavior.

4. *personal*

5. because he did so many things he didn't want to do

6. to keep other people from finding it out

7. because he hadn't taken a drink

8. no/he smashed his car, lost his suit, a hundred dollars, and his wristwatch; and he lost his sobriety

9. "So long as I'm thinking as I'm thinking now, and so long as I'm doing as I'm doing now, I don't believe I'll ever take another drink."

10. that I should ask to know God's will for me for that day, and then, to the best of my ability, to follow that, and at night to express my gratefulness to God for the things that had happened to me during the day

PIONEERS OF AA "Women Suffer Too"

1. they were no longer her friends/*personal*

2. *personal*

3. her inability to accept the harsh realities of life

4. she needed it to keep going; she didn't feel comfortable around other people without drinking.

5. she discovered she wasn't the only person in the world who felt and behaved like this

6. religion

7. freedom

8. she wasn't alone anymore

9. more and more she put into practice the Twelve Steps

THEY STOPPED IN TIME "Too Young?"

1. no

2. *personal*

3. *personal*

4. thought he was too young

5. to help him get sober and stay sober themselves

6. when he started to take AA seriously

THEY STOPPED IN TIME "Fear of Fear"

1. she got in trouble

2. she didn't want to be a drunk/*personal*

3. her self-respect

4. she couldn't face people, she hid, she wouldn't answer the phone, she avoided friends

5. *personal*

6. they now have faith in each other, trust in each other, and understanding

7. because they are the build-up of another drunk

8. her sobriety and her ability to help other people

THEY STOPPED IN TIME "A Teenager's Decision"

1. she drank as often and as much as she could

2. because she had been unhappy, lonely, and scared for so long

3. no/hangovers, blackouts, car accident; she lost her

license, was made a ward of the court, was put on probation, ran away, didn't graduate from high school, hurt her parents, hated herself, lost her friends

4. the more she drank, the worse it got and the more she had to drink

5. she knew she didn't want to live if life was going to go on like it was

6. the freedom of truth/admitting she was an alcoholic

7. she/by taking the first drink

THEY LOST NEARLY ALL "A Five-Time Loser Wins"

1. one's personality/*personal*

2. our good intentions dissolved

3. by going to many AA meetings with an open mind and a desire to live the good-feeling life without chemicals

4. kill the old self/build a new, free self

5. the living hell before death

6. He surrendered totally

7. there's more to sobriety than abstinence; sobriety involves a change of personality and a spiritual awakening

8. AA and God

9. I want to be sober and in AA

THEY LOST NEARLY ALL "Freedom from Bondage"

1. I am the result of the way I reacted to what happened to me as a child

2. the only thing that changed was her surroundings/herself

3. a spiritual hunger

4. false/because it did not come from within her

5. *personal*

6. grim/pleasant

7. honesty, openness, willingness

8. get us sober and keep us sober

9. by the contrast between her plans for her life and what had really happened

10. *personal*

11. doing what you ought to do because you want to do it

THEY LOST NEARLY ALL "AA Taught Him to Handle Sobriety"

1. to stay stopped

2. he read self-help books, he turned to religion with a fervor, he swore off hard liquor and turned to wine, he sneaked drinks, he drank in the morning

3. his ability to lie outwardly and kid himself inwardly

4. when he was criticized or reprimanded/*personal*

5. because he failed to live up to his own expectations of himself

6. *personal*

7. through practicing the Twelve Steps and through sharing at meetings

8. as we begin to live in the present, one day at a time

9. fantasizing/reality

10. it taught him to relate to people, to deal with disappointments and problems, that the name of the game is to stay sober

"SPIRITUAL EXPERIENCE"

1. manifested itself among us in many different forms

2. that personality changes must be in the nature of sudden and spectacular upheavals

3. the "educational variety" because they develop slowly over a period of time

4. an unsuspected inner resource which they presently identify with their own conception of a Power greater than themselves

5. this awareness of a Power greater than ourselves

6. he does not close his mind to spiritual concepts

7. willingness, honesty, and open-mindedness

8. if we've closed our mind to something before checking it out, we'll stay ignorant

About the Author

John Rosengren grew up in Wayzata, Minnesota, earned a B.A. in English at St. John's University, Collegeville, Minnesota, wrote short stories in Paris, and worked as a chemical dependency counselor in an adolescent treatment center near Boise, Idaho. He now works as a free-lance writer in Minneapolis. He has published a collection of short stories on teenage addiction, *Life Is Just a Party: Portrait of a Teenage Partier,* and many articles about teenage drug abuse and prevention. He is recovering from chemical dependency and frequently speaks in schools about sports, drugs, and self-esteem.